The Usborne
Story of London
Picture Book

Rob Lloyd Jones

Illustrated by Princesse Camcam

Designed by Hannah Ahmed and Caroline Day

Edited by Jane Chisholm

Contents

Welcome to London

One of the biggest and most exciting cities in the world, London is crammed with fascinating things to see. This map shows the busy heart of the city, where you'll find most of the famous places in this book.

London Zoo

British Museum

The British Museum is full of priceless objects from the past – including Ancient Egyptian mummies and illuminated medieval manuscripts.

British Museum

Nelson's Column

This stone monument, topped with a statue of naval hero Admiral Lord Nelson, rises from the middle of bustling Trafalgar Square.

Marble Arch

Piccadilly Circus

Marble Arch

You can find out more about this grand stone gateway on page 19.

Trafalgar Square

Buckingham Palace

This luxurious palace is the Queen's official home in London.

Houses of Parliament

Politicians meet here to debate important issues about the country. The famous Clock Tower is known as Big Ben.

The River Thames

Hyde Park

London Eye

Buckingham Palace

Houses of Parliament

Westminster Abbey

London Eye

This huge observation wheel offers passengers spectacular views across London.

Westminster Abbey

For over 1,000 years, British kings and queens have been crowned at this magnificent old monastery church.

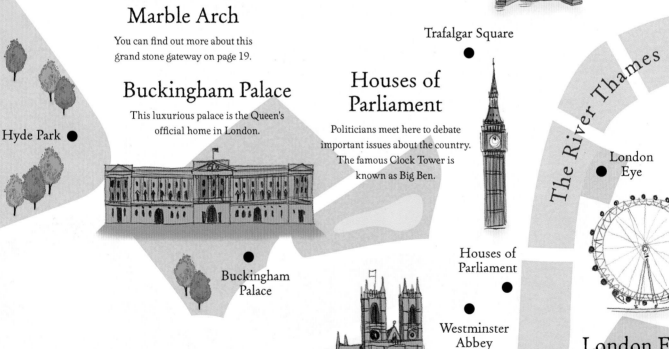

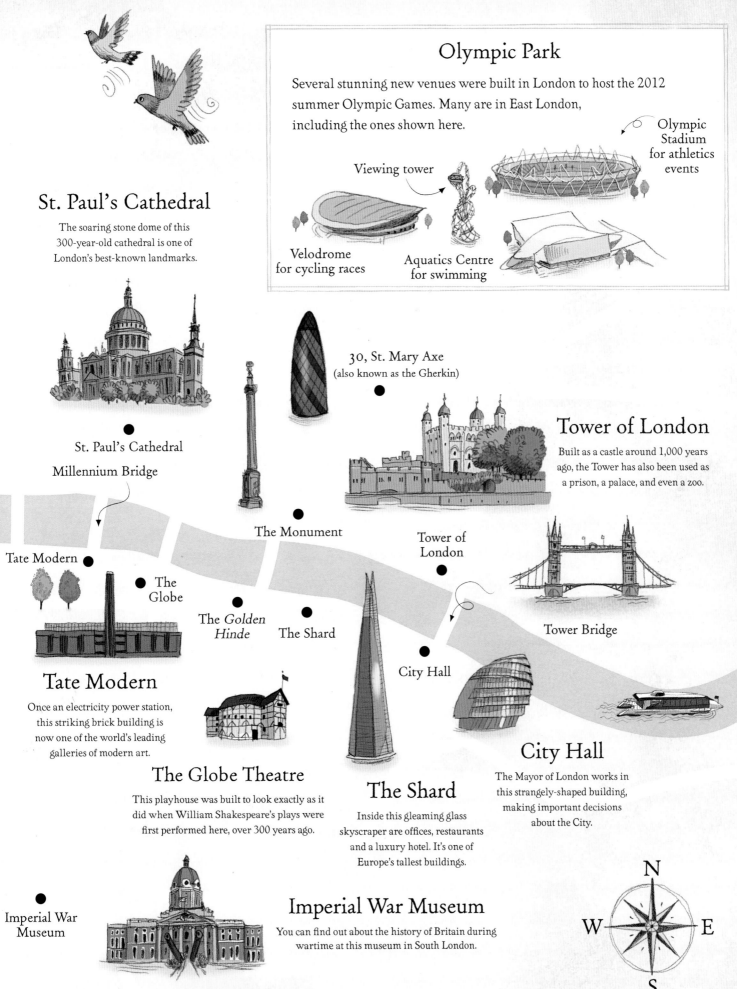

Olympic Park

Several stunning new venues were built in London to host the 2012 summer Olympic Games. Many are in East London, including the ones shown here.

Viewing tower

Olympic Stadium for athletics events

Velodrome for cycling races

Aquatics Centre for swimming

St. Paul's Cathedral

The soaring stone dome of this 300-year-old cathedral is one of London's best-known landmarks.

St. Paul's Cathedral

Millennium Bridge

30, St. Mary Axe (also known as the Gherkin)

Tower of London

Built as a castle around 1,000 years ago, the Tower has also been used as a prison, a palace, and even a zoo.

The Monument

Tower of London

Tate Modern

The Globe

The *Golden Hinde*

The Shard

City Hall

Tower Bridge

Tate Modern

Once an electricity power station, this striking brick building is now one of the world's leading galleries of modern art.

The Globe Theatre

This playhouse was built to look exactly as it did when William Shakespeare's plays were first performed here, over 300 years ago.

The Shard

Inside this gleaming glass skyscraper are offices, restaurants and a luxury hotel. It's one of Europe's tallest buildings.

City Hall

The Mayor of London works in this strangely-shaped building, making important decisions about the City.

Imperial War Museum

Imperial War Museum

You can find out about the history of Britain during wartime at this museum in South London.

N
W   E
S

The beginning...

Around 2,000 years ago, the Romans invaded Britain. They built a bridge over the River Thames, and a fort to guard it. A large town grew beside the fort. The Romans named it Londinium.

Roman Londinium

Londinium was home to over 20,000 people. There were temples, bath houses, and a bustling market square. Trading ships arrived at the town's busy port, bringing luxuries from around the Roman Empire.

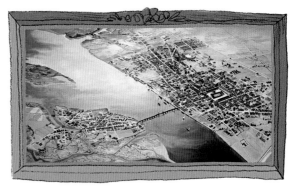

This is how Londinium looked around the year 120.

Rich Romans

Londinium became a prosperous place, where wealthy people decorated their houses with intricate mosaics, like this one showing a Roman god riding a tiger.

People from Londinium flocked to the stadium at the edge of town, where they watched armed fighters, called gladiators, battle to the death.

Gladiators often wore heavy bronze helmets like this one, which were decorated with symbols of strength and victory.

Under attack!

In the year 60, the Romans were attacked by a tribe of warriors called the Iceni, led by Queen Boudicca. They set fire to Londinium, slaughtering thousands of its citizens. Eventually, Boudicca was defeated, and the city was rebuilt.

After Boudicca's attack, the Romans built a wall around Londinium to protect it against enemy tribes.

Today, this bronze statue of Boudicca on her chariot stands beside the River Thames, in Westminster.

The Middle Ages

The Romans left Britain in around 500, and for a long time the city was almost empty. It became busy again in around 750, when it was settled by Vikings from Scandinavia. By the 1300s, London (as it was then known), had grown into a large city – with a stone cathedral, and new, stronger city walls.

There were over 100 churches in London then, but the biggest was St. Paul's Cathedral. This model shows how it looked in 1320 – very different from today.

During the Middle Ages, a lot of the land in London was taken up by monasteries. Monks lived and prayed there, and gave out food to the poor.

Hustle and bustle

Every shop owner belonged to one of the city's guilds – powerful groups that set prices and protected traders' rights. Members gathered at the Guildhall, where meetings were led by the Lord Mayor of London.

The Guildhall was built in the 1400s, although only parts of the original hall remain today. Its grand interior is used for banquets and balls.

Traders often displayed their guild emblem on their shop front. This sign was for the Company of Grocers, who made sure spices were bought and sold fairly.

In the Middle Ages, London's streets were often named after the jobs people did there. Some of the names still survive today...

Tailors worked in...

THREADNEEDLE STREET

Cows were kept in...

MILK STREET

Bakers worked in...

BREAD STREET

Westminster Abbey

One of London's oldest and grandest buildings, Westminster Abbey was built in the Middle Ages as a church for a monastery.

The first abbey in Westminster was built around 1,000 years ago, by King Edward the Confessor. Monks lived in the church, and farmed the fields around it. Then, in 1245, King Henry III rebuilt the church in a much grander style. Work continued for around 500 years.

This scene, painted by the Italian artist Canaletto in 1749, shows a procession of knights entering the Abbey.

You can see this carving of a king, and lots of others like it, above the Abbey's Great North Door.

Most of the new Abbey was built in a style known as Gothic that was popular in the Middle Ages. The outsides are decorated with stone carvings of kings, angels and saints.

Visitors come and go through the North Entrance.

Many English kings and queens are buried here, in King Henry VII's Chapel.

The Abbey's two bell towers were designed in the 1700s, by architect Nicholas Hawksmoor.

This is the Chapter House, where monks met each day to read a chapter of the Bible.

Stone 'buttresses' along the outside support the weight of the Abbey's vaulted ceiling.

Royal ceremonies

Since 1066, all Britain's kings and queens have been crowned at the Abbey in glittering ceremonies. Royal funerals and weddings are sometimes held there, too.

In April 2011, the Duke and Duchess of Cambridge were married in the Abbey. Around two billion people watched the service on television around the world.

King Henry IV was crowned in the Abbey in 1399. This painting, from a medieval manuscript, shows his coronation ceremony.

During coronation ceremonies, the king or queen sits on this wooden Coronation Chair. Carved in 1297, it was once covered in gold leaf. There's a space under the seat, where a stone slab, called the Stone of Scone, is inserted before every coronation. The stone symbolizes the monarch's rule over Scotland.

The four gilded lions that support the Coronation Chair were added in the 1700s.

Inside the Abbey

Westminster Abbey's vast interior is lavishly decorated with paintings, stained glass windows, and high-vaulted ceilings carved in intricate patterns.

This beautiful window shows King Henry III (on the left). On the right is Richard de Ware, the Abbot (head monk) of Westminster during the 13th century.

Tombs and memorials

Most of Britain's kings and queens are buried in the Abbey, as well as hundreds of other important figures from British history – artists, scientists, politicians and military leaders. Many of them are commemorated with plaques, stained glass windows, or statues.

The Tomb of the Unknown Warrior remembers soldiers who died during the First World War.

Poets' Corner has stone memorials to famous British writers, including Geoffrey Chaucer and Charles Dickens.

This memorial to William Shakespeare was added to Poets' Corner in 1740.

Tudor London

From 1485, England was ruled by the Tudor kings and queens. In Tudor times, London became one of the biggest cities in the world. Almost 200,000 people lived among its dirty, rowdy, tightly-packed streets.

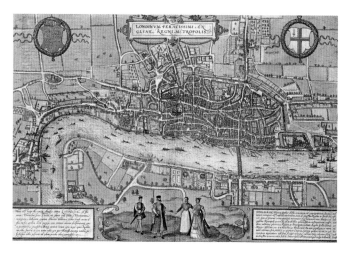

This is the first printed map of London, made in 1572. It shows the City of London (around London Bridge) and the village of Westminster further west. Today, all the green fields on the map are part of London too.

Finished in 1536, St. James's Palace was home to most of the Tudor kings and queens, including Henry VIII and Elizabeth I. Its imposing 16th-century red-brick gatehouse still survives today.

There were around 200 houses and shops, up to seven floors high, on London Bridge.

In those days, London Bridge was the only bridge across the Thames. Its base was so wide it stopped the river from flowing fast. So, the water often froze in winter and 'frost fairs' were held on the thick ice.

The modern Globe Theatre was built using the same materials and techniques as the original playhouse.

Playhouses

The Tudor period was a golden age for music, theatre and arts in Britain. This was especially true of London, where people flocked to playhouses. One of the most famous was the Globe, south of the river, which was partly owned by the playwright William Shakespeare.

Around 3,000 people packed into the Globe at a time. If they didn't like the play, they threw fruit at the stage.

Shakespeare came to London from Stratford-upon-Avon in around 1590, joining a group of actors, called the Lord Chamberlain's Men. Many of his plays, such as *Romeo and Juliet*, *Hamlet* and *Macbeth*, were first performed at the Globe, and other London playhouses.

Today you can see this replica of the *Golden Hinde* on the South bank, near London Bridge.

Street life

London's narrow streets could be dangerous. Pickpockets prowled among the crowds, and drunken men stumbled from rowdy taverns, often getting into fights.

Each tavern had a stone sign hanging outside. This one belonged to the *Boar's Head Tavern*, near London Bridge.

River life

Small boats ferried people up and down the river, and trading ships arrived at London's crowded docks. Other ships set off on epic journeys, like that of explorer Sir Francis Drake, who sailed around the world in the *Golden Hinde*, from 1577 to 1588.

Most of London's streets were littered with rubbish and awash with reeking toilet waste. Some people carried bottles of perfume, like this one, to help combat the foul smells.

The Tower of London

This famous fortress beside the Thames was built as a castle, over 900 years ago, by King William the Conqueror. Since then, the Tower has had many different uses...

This medieval manuscript is one of the oldest paintings of the Tower. It shows the Duke of Orleans, a French noble, imprisoned inside. Unlike many of the Tower's prisoners, the Duke was released unharmed, in 1440.

Off with their heads!

During Tudor times, especially, parts of the Tower were used as prison cells.

This painting shows the execution of Lady Jane Grey in the Tower, in 1554. She was sentenced to death for treason by Queen Mary I.

The Tower of London is actually made up of 21 towers, surrounded by thick stone walls. The oldest and largest part is the White Tower – given its name in the 1400s, when it was painted white.

Some of the Tower's prisoners had their heads chopped off using this block and axe. Henry VIII's second wife, Anne Boleyn, was executed there in 1536. Some people say her ghost still haunts the castle...

Some prisoners were brought to the Tower by boat.

Seven ravens are kept as pets in the Tower's grounds. One legend says that if the birds ever leave, the Tower will fall – and so will all of England.

Since the 1500s, the Tower has been guarded by Yeoman Warders, also known as Beefeaters (possibly because they were once paid with meat). Nowadays, they give tours, dressed in their traditional red and gold, or red and black, uniforms.

This silver engraved armour belonged to King Henry VIII.

Royal collections

Over the centuries, the Tower has stored all sorts of valuable things belonging to the royal family.

Since the 1300s, the priceless 'Crown Jewels' have been kept in the Tower. These are crowns, sceptres and golden orbs, used in royal ceremonies.

The Imperial State Crown, worn by British monarchs for their coronations, is decorated with 23,578 dazzling jewels.

Weapons for war were kept in the Royal Armoury – swords, rifles and gleaming suits of armour.

A polar bear lived in the Tower in the Middle Ages. It swam in the Thames to catch fish.

From the Middle Ages, the Tower was also used as a zoo for exotic animals, including tigers, kangaroos and bears. In 1830, two cages were accidentally left open, causing a savage fight between tigers and a lion. Two years later, the animals were moved to a new home at London Zoo.

Plague & Fire

From 1665 to 1666, disaster struck London. First, a deadly plague ravaged the city, killing thousands. Then a fire broke out that left much of London in smoking ruins.

The plague was spread by fleas carried on black rats.

This drawing from the 1600s shows the plague as a skeleton, dancing on coffins and hurling arrows at London's fleeing citizens. On the right, people from other towns warn infected Londoners to stay away.

Some doctors brave enough to visit plague victims tried to guard against the disease by wearing long leather robes and masks with 'beaks' stuffed with herbs. They thought these would protect them.

This engraving, from 1656, shows the typical clothing of a plague doctor.

Plague victims were locked in their homes, with a red cross painted on the door.

Whenever plague victims were buried, a 'plague bell' (such as the one on the left) was rung. The sound reminded people to take precautions against spreading the disease.

Dead bodies were piled in carts and buried in deep 'plague pits' outside the city.

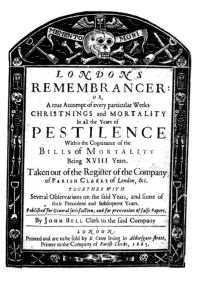

The plague ravaged London for over a year, killing around 68,000 people. This is the front page from a 'bill of mortality', a weekly record of the city's dead.

The Great Fire

On September 2, 1666, a fire broke out in a baker's shop on Pudding Lane, near London Bridge. Most of the city's buildings were made of wood and crammed close together. So, fanned by fierce winds, the flames quickly spread.

Firemen battled to fight the fire, using wooden pumps filled with water from the Thames.

This scene, painted around 1667, shows the Great Fire engulfing St. Paul's Cathedral, as London burns.

City in ruins

The Great Fire of London lasted for four terrible days, destroying over 13,000 homes, and leaving St. Paul's in ruins. But, amazingly, only nine people are reported to have died.

People crowded into boats to escape the flames. Some thought the Fire was a punishment from God.

In 1677, the Monument was built to commemorate the Fire – a stone column with a golden urn at the top to symbolize flames. Sculptures around its base show King Charles II planning to rebuild the city.

Remembering the Fire

A golden statue of a boy marks the spot where the Fire ended. As it raged from Pudding Lane to Pie Corner, some believed it was God's punishment for overeating. That's why the boy holds his full stomach.

You can see the Golden Boy on Giltspur Street, in the City (Pie Corner no longer exists).

After the Fire

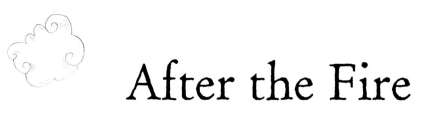

London was quickly rebuilt and grew into a place of great wealth and new ideas. In 1714, George I became king, and the next 100 years is known as the Georgian Period.

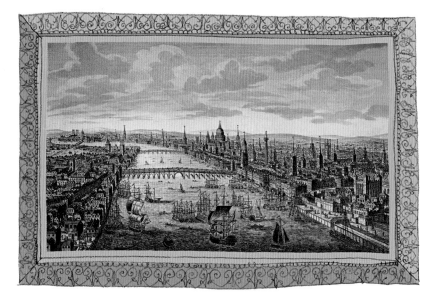

Looking down the river from the east, this is London's skyline almost 100 years after the Fire. The houses that burned down were rebuilt in brick, with wide streets, to stop fires from spreading so easily again.

Elegant new streets, such as Regent Street and Piccadilly, were built in London's 'West End'. These were fashionable places, where wealthy ladies promenaded in elaborate silk dresses, while men wore bright velvet coats and powdered wigs.

This doll's house, from 1760, shows the type of 'townhouse' in which many rich Londoners lived. Often these grand homes were laid out around private gardens in elegant squares.

On one day each year, from 1757, the Lord Mayor of the City of London paraded the streets in this dazzling golden coach, pulled by six horses. Today, you can see the coach in the Museum of London.

14

Work and play

Several scientific institutions were founded in London, such as the Royal Society, and the Royal Observatory, in Greenwich, on the right. Completed in 1675, it was used by astronomers for studying the night sky.

Astronomers at the Observatory charted the positions of stars to help sailors navigate at sea.

Pleasure gardens – private parks, where people came to dance, drink and gossip – became fashionable, although only the rich could afford the entry fees. This poster advertised Vauxhall Royal Gardens.

Each year, in May, a fair was held in Greenwich Park. People drank, and danced and ran arm-in-arm down the steep slope. In 1857, the fair was shut down for becoming too rowdy.

Down and out

While the rich enjoyed the high life, many poor people lived in crowded slums. The most desperate turned to crime. Nightwatchmen patrolled the streets, looking out for thieves. If you were caught, you might be sent to the notorious Newgate Prison.

Nightwatchmen carried lanterns and wooden staffs as they paced London's streets.

This print, from 1791, shows the forbidding entrance to Newgate Prison. The infamous jail was demolished in 1902.

Landmarks of Georgian London

Grand designs

Banqueting House, in Westminster, was completed in 1622, but its design influenced a lot of 18th century London architecture. Its architect, Inigo Jones, copied ancient Greek and Roman styles, with elegant stone columns.

Georgian houses often have semi-circular windows, called fanlights, above the doors.

You can still see lots of Georgian houses in London, especially in Bloomsbury, near the British Museum. They usually have arched doorways. Look out for blue plaques outside. This means a famous person once lived there.

Kensington Palace was a private mansion, until William III turned it into his palace in 1689. During the 1700s, it was extended, and became the home of several British monarchs. Diana, Princess of Wales, lived there. Her memorial is in nearby Kensington Gardens.

A statue of King William III stands outside the Palace.

Fortnum & Mason

This spectacular clock decorates the outside of Fortnum & Mason, an exclusive department store on Piccadilly, which has sold goods to London's high society for over 300 years. Each hour, models of the founders, William Fortnum and Hugh Mason, emerge from behind doors and greet each other with a bow.

At Christmas, some of Fortnum & Mason's mail-order goods are still delivered by horse and carriage.

16

Samuel Johnson

Author Samuel Johnson became one of the most famous people in Georgian London when he published one of the first ever dictionaries in 1755. Johnson's house is now a museum, where you can find out more about his life and times.

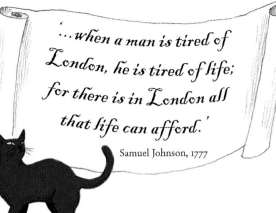

'...when a man is tired of London, he is tired of life; for there is in London all that life can afford.'

Samuel Johnson, 1777

This statue of Johnson stands on the Strand, near his old house. Outside the house you can also see a statue of the author's beloved cat, Hodge.

Wren's London

Many of London's grandest new buildings were designed by Sir Christopher Wren, an astronomer, mathematician and architect. On the left is the spire of St. Bride's, on Fleet Street, one of 52 churches that Wren built in the city. Its stepped shape may have influenced the design of wedding cakes. Wren's most famous church was St. Paul's Cathedral.

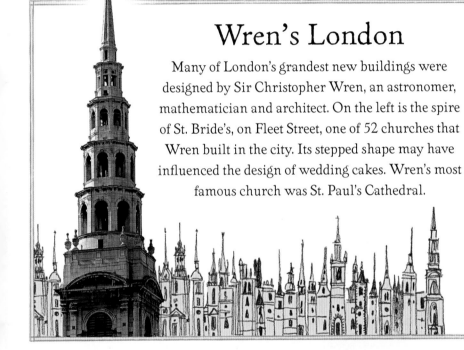

Wren designed this stone arch, known as Temple Bar, which once stood over Fleet Street, as a gateway to the City of London. In 2003, it was re-erected close to St. Paul's Cathedral.

Royal parks

Many of London's parks, such as Green Park and St. James's Park, are known as 'royal parks'. This is because they were originally built for the royal family on private land, before the parks became public in the 1700s.

Parks were fashionable places to be seen, and also where gentlemen met for deadly duels.

This is the elegant lake and bridge (called the Blue Bridge) in St. James's Park.

St. Paul's Cathedral

The Cathedral ceilings are decorated with dazzling mosaics, made of over 30 million pieces of glass.

The soaring dome of St. Paul's Cathedral is one of London's most famous landmarks. Religious services are held there, and around 3 million people visit every year.

After the old cathedral was destroyed in the Great Fire, Sir Christopher Wren designed a new St. Paul's. Built from white Portland stone, it was completed in 1710.

A golden statue of St. Paul with a cross stands on a column outside the Cathedral.

St. Paul's rises above the city, in this detail from a scene painted in 1748 by Italian artist Canaletto. The boats on the Thames are celebrating Lord Mayor's Day.

This image of Christopher Wren is from a window of another church he designed, St. Lawrence Jewry, close to St. Paul's.

The dome is one of the largest in the world. It's actually two domes, one inside the other, with a brick 'cone' between them to support their weight.

An arched crypt runs underneath, where you can see the tombs of famous people, including military heroes Admiral Lord Nelson (above) and the Duke of Wellington.

Buckingham Palace

This magnificent palace in the heart of London has been the official home of British kings and queens since 1837.

Once the home of a duke, 'Buckingham House' was rebuilt from 1826 as a royal palace. In 1837, Queen Victoria became the first monarch to move in. Before that, kings and queens lived in St. James's Palace.

On national days of celebration, the Royal Family sometimes gather on the Palace's central balcony, to wave at cheering crowds.

This golden symbol is the official coat of arms of the monarch. You can see it on the ornate iron gates that guard the Palace forecourt.

The Palace is guarded by 'Foot Guards', who wear red jackets and furry helmets called bearskins. Every day in the summer, you can watch a parade called 'Changing the Guard'.

A wide ceremonial road, called the Mall, leads to the Palace. It's lined with trees, and sometimes flags too.

If you spot this flag, the Royal Standard, flying over the Palace, that means the Queen is at home. Maybe she's having a cup of tea...

This stone gateway, known as 'Marble Arch', used to be the main entrance to Buckingham Palace. It was taken away in 1851, and now stands at the western end of Oxford Street.

Victorian London

Queen Victoria became queen in 1837. During her 63-year reign, London grew into the biggest, richest city in the world – the beating heart of a mighty empire that stretched around the globe.

Great wealth...

This painting, by John O'Connor, shows the north bank of the Thames in 1874, with the broad new 'Embankment' running along the riverside. Factory chimneys dot the skyline, and a steam train chugs across Blackfriars Bridge.

The world's first railways were built in London in the 1830s. Now people could work in the city, but live further out. So London grew even bigger.

In 1851, a huge exhibition in London showed off Britain's industrial might. *The Great Exhibition of Industry of All Nations* was held in Hyde Park, inside a vast glass and steel structure called the Crystal Palace. Around 6 million people came to marvel at displays of new technology.

This engraving shows Chinese sailors unloading a tea ship at one of London's busy docks.

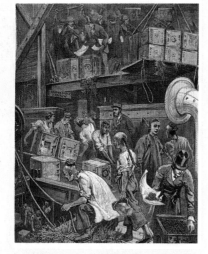

Profits from the Exhibition's entry tickets were used to build new museums in London, including the Victoria and Albert Museum, and the Natural History Museum.

Like many public buildings in the Victorian period, the Natural History Museum was built in a medieval Gothic style (see page 23).

Trading ships jostled for space at London's docks, bringing goods, such as tea, from as far as China. Immigrants arrived on these ships too, and so the city became home to people from all over the world.

...and grim poverty

Between 1800 and 1900, London's population grew four times bigger, as people moved to the city to work in its factories. Many of these people were paid very low wages, so the richest city in the world also became home to shocking levels of poverty.

Even children as young as ten scraped a living on London's streets...

Factories belched brown fumes into the air, causing thick fogs of pollution to engulf the city.

Flower girls

Shoeblacks shined people's shoes.

Crossing sweepers cleared horse muck from people's paths.

Mudlarks scoured the riverbanks, scavenging for things to sell.

The author Charles Dickens, one of the most famous Londoners of the 19th century, vividly described the struggles of the city's poor in novels such as *Oliver Twist* and *Little Dorrit*.

Many poor people lived in squalid areas known as slums. Sometimes, whole families shared just one decrepit room. One of the worst slums in the city was Seven Dials – today it's a fashionable shopping district near Covent Garden.

This scene, painted by Luke Fildes in 1874, shows desperate families queueing for a free meal outside a London workhouse.

Many poor people took their drinking water from the Thames, which was so polluted it caused diseases. This newspaper cartoon depicts the figure of Death pumping water for them to drink.

With so many people crammed together, diseases such as cholera spread rapidly. From the 1850s, new sewers were laid across the city, to help make it cleaner.

Landmarks of Victorian London

Trafalgar Square

This famous public square was completed in 1844, to celebrate a great naval victory at Trafalgar in 1805. Around 15 million people visit each year, making it the fourth most popular tourist site in the world.

A statue of Admiral Lord Nelson, who led the victory at Trafalgar, stands on top of a 46m (150ft) high column.

Four bronze lions guard the base of Nelson's Column. They are made from metal from the cannons of old battleships.

On one side of Trafalgar Square is the National Gallery, which opened in 1838. It's free to go inside, to see over 2,300 paintings by the most famous names in the history of art.

Temple Bar Memorial

This striking bronze dragon stands in the middle of Fleet Street, opposite the Royal Courts of Justice. Erected in 1880, it marks the spot where Temple Bar once stood (see page 17). On one side of the dragon's tall plinth is a statue of Queen Victoria. On the other side is her son, the Prince of Wales, who became King Edward VII in 1901.

The Temple Bar Memorial was designed by Sir Horace Jones. The dragon is the official symbol of the City of London.

Victoria & Albert

After Queen Victoria's husband, Prince Albert, died in 1861, several monuments were dedicated to him. The most famous is the Royal Albert Hall, an oval concert hall in Kensington. It opened in 1871, and hosts music concerts, and dance shows.

Just cross the road is this elaborate monument, the Albert Memorial. In the middle is a statue of the Prince covered in gold leaf, and surrounded by marble sculptures, and mosaics.

Victorian Gothic

Many Victorian buildings were designed in a grand medieval style, known as Victorian Gothic. The front of St. Pancras Station, designed by George Gilbert Scott, is a good example, with jagged spires, and decorated arches. Completed in 1873, it is both a station and a grand hotel.

Today, Eurostar trains from Europe arrive at St. Pancras Station.

Tower Bridge

London's most famous bridge was completed in 1894, and remains the only one that opens up. Around 1,000 times a year, traffic across the bridge is stopped, as the middle sections (called bascules) rise to let tall ships pass through.

The Houses of Parliament

The Houses of Parliament, also known as the Palace of Westminster, is one of the most important buildings in Britain. It's where politicians meet to agree new laws, and debate vital issues about the country.

Guy Fawkes

This engraving, made shortly after the Gunpowder Plot, shows Guy Fawkes (in the middle) with his fellow plotters.

Gunpowder plot

On November 5, 1605, a man named Guy Fawkes tried to blow up Parliament, using gunpowder hidden in the cellar. Fawkes wanted to kill King James I, who was making a speech there. But he was caught in the act. Every year in Britain, the 'Gunpowder Plot' is remembered with bonfires and fireworks.

Then, in 1834, the Houses of Parliament were destroyed by an accidental fire. A new building was designed by architect Sir Charles Barry in a dramatic 'Gothic' style, mimicking the look of nearby Westminster Abbey. It was completed in 1868.

The old Palace of Westminster is shown engulfed in flames in this scene painted by J.M.W. Turner in 1834.

Parts of the Houses of Parliament are decorated with stone carvings. This lion is a symbol of royalty.

If a flag is flying from the top of this tower, it means that politicians are meeting inside.

Westminster Hall is the oldest bit of the site. It's all that is left of a medieval palace that once stood here.

The Clock Tower

Riverside restaurant for politicians

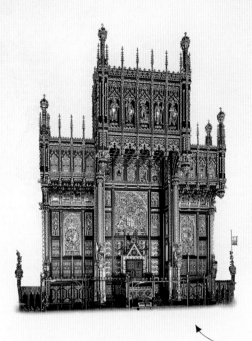

Inside the Palace

Inside are over 5km (3 miles) of corridors, as well as 100 flights of stairs, and around 1,100 rooms. Many of the rooms were designed by architect Augustus Pugin, with beautiful stained glass, decorated floor tiles, and patterned wallpapers.

Elaborate wooden panels adorn the walls of some of Parliament's rooms. This one, from the House of Lords, is painted with the symbol of Parliament (a portcullis and a crown), as well as emblems of royalty.

Once a year, the Queen sits on this Ceremonial Throne for the 'Opening of Parliament'.

No. 10

When British Prime Ministers go to Parliament, they only have to travel down the road. Nearby, No.10 Downing Street has been the home to Prime Ministers since 1735. The famous front door looks as if it's made of wood, but is in fact thick steel, to withstand terrorist attacks.

Inside Parliament is the House of Lords, and the House of Commons, where the Prime Minister and other politicians debate important issues.

DING DONG, DING DONG!

The Clock Tower's largest bell (Big Ben) is so heavy that 16 horses were needed to drag it on a carriage to Westminster, in 1858.

Big Ben

Parliament's clock tower, also designed by Pugin, is the most famous in the world. It's often called Big Ben, but, actually, that's the nickname of a huge bronze bell inside the tower. No one knows who the bell was named after. It might have been Sir Benjamin Hall, who oversaw the rebuilding of Parliament.

London at war

London came under attack during the 20th century, in the devastating air raids of the First and Second World Wars. Bombs fell, fires raged, and parts of the city were left in ruins.

First strikes

During the First World War, German airships loomed over London, loaded with bombs. The first air raid came in May 1915, and there were around 50 more attacks on London and other cities. The Germans hoped they would destroy British morale, but they made those affected even more determined to win.

IT IS FAR BETTER TO FACE THE BULLETS THAN TO BE KILLED AT HOME BY A BOMB

JOIN THE ARMY AT ONCE & HELP TO STOP AN AIR RAID

GOD SAVE THE KING

During the First World War, recruitment posters like this urged Londoners to fight back by joining the army.

St. Paul's Cathedral stands among smoke from the bombs, in this famous photograph taken in December 1940, during the Blitz.

Powerful searchlights scoured London's sky, looking for enemy planes. Air raid sirens warned Londoners of an attack.

The Blitz

London came under attack again in the Second World War, in a series of air raids between September 1940 and May 1941, known as the Blitz. German aircraft dropped thousands of bombs over the city, killing over 20,000 people.

For protection, thousands of children were evacuated from London. Many were sent to live with complete strangers in the countryside.

LEAVE THIS TO US SONNY — YOU OUGHT TO BE OUT OF LONDON

MINISTRY OF HEALTH EVACUATION SCHEME

This poster encouraged parents to send their children away from the city.

During the Blitz, Londoners followed strict safety rules, such as covering their windows with black cloth at night, so that enemy bombers couldn't spot house lights to aim at. Air Raid Wardens kept watch over the city, making sure that everyone obeyed these rules.

War memorials

There are lots of memorials in London to remember victims of war. This is the most famous one, the Cenotaph, in Westminster.

Each year, on the Sunday closest to November 11, the anniversary of the end of the First World War, a service is held at the Cenotaph. Politicians, military veterans, and the Royal Family lay poppy wreaths to remember people who died in wars.

This bronze sculpture, near St. Paul's Cathedral, pays tribute to firefighters who died in the Blitz.

War museums

Now permanantly docked near Tower Bridge is *HMS Belfast*, a warship which took part in the 1944 invasion of France during the Second World War. It's now a museum, where you can learn more about the British Royal Navy.

At the Imperial War Museum, you can see planes, such as this *Supermarine Spitfire* fighter, which defended London against German bombers during the Blitz.

As bombs fell during the Second World War, the British government met in secret headquarters, the Cabinet War Rooms, deep beneath the streets of Westminster. You can visit these rooms today.

London today

Around 12 million people live in London today. The city is a pulsating mix of old and new. Monuments from its turbulent past sit proudly beside dazzling new buildings.

Modern marvels

Completed in 2012, the Shard, near London Bridge, is London's tallest building. Its shape, and glass casing, make it resemble a 'shard of glass'.

Passengers on the London Eye view London from inside 32 glass capsules.

Rising over the River Thames, the London Eye is a huge observation wheel built to celebrate the new millennium. Each glass capsule takes about 30 minutes to go around, giving amazing views across the city.

The Shard is 310m (1,017ft) high. Its 87 floors include offices, private apartments, a luxury hotel, and, at the top, a viewing gallery for the public.

The Lloyd's Building, home to the insurance company Lloyd's of London, was designed by architect Richard Rogers and finished in 1986. Rogers put the building's elevators and pipes on the outside, so there's more room inside for offices.

30, St. Mary Axe was finished in 2003, and is often called 'the Gherkin', because of its distinctive shape. Inside are mostly offices, but there's also a restaurant at the top.

Although the building is curved, each of its 7,429 glass panes is flat, except for the one at the very top.

Around 600 people – including the Mayor of London – work in this gleaming glass building, City Hall, beside the Thames. Together, they make important decisions about the future of the city.

Art and culture

London has dozens of museums and galleries, many of which are free to visit. The Tate Modern is one of the most popular. It was an old power station that closed in 1981, and now displays modern art from all over the world.

At the heart of the British Museum is the stunning Great Court, and a huge round library, or Reading Room.

The Tate Modern is on the south bank of the River Thames, directly opposite St. Paul's Cathedral.

Around 6 million people visit the British Museum every year. It has 8 million objects from throughout history, including Ancient Egyptian mummies, and Greek sculptures.

City of the world

People from all over the globe have made London their home. Around 300 languages are spoken there – more than in any other city in the world. This brightly decorated gateway is in a bustling area known as Chinatown, home to many of London's Chinese community.

Each year, around the end of January, acrobats, musicians and dancing dragons parade through Chinatown, to celebrate the start of the Chinese New Year.

Many of London's streets and squares are famous all around the world...

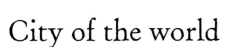

PICCADILLY CIRCUS W1
CITY OF WESTMINSTER

...is at the heart of London's theatre district. You can spot this statue of a Greek god, often called Eros.

The Royal Borough of Kensington and Chelsea
PORTOBELLO ROAD, W.11

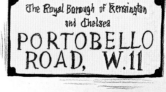

This street is famous for its market, which sells vintage clothes, and antiques.

THEATRELAND
COVENT GARDEN WC2
CITY OF WESTMINSTER

...is an old market turned into a buzzy shopping area, where you can see street artists perform.

OXFORD STREET W.1
City of Westminster

...is Europe's busiest shopping street, packed with around 300 shops.

London transport

L ondon has one of the largest public transport systems in the world. Every day, around 6.5 million people travel on trains, underground trains, and buses.

Double deckers

Around 150 years ago, London's streets were clogged with carriages. From 1829, horse-pulled 'omnibuses' carried passengers on two decks. The top decks had no roofs, so people paid more to sit below, where it was warmer.

This 'double-decker' omnibus, from 1875, carries advertisements – just as buses do today.

This double-decker bus is from the 1920s. Passengers climbed stairs at the back to the top deck.

By 1900, omnibuses, or 'buses' as they became known, were powered by engines, and often painted red.

Today, red double-decker buses are recognized as a symbol of London. Every day around 7,500 buses carry passengers through the city.

This is how some of London's double-decker buses look today.

Taxi!

If you wanted to ride alone in Victorian London, you could pay a driver to carry you in his black, horse-drawn 'hansom cab'.

An orange sign on the top lights up when the cab is available for hire.

Today, there are around 20,000 black cabs (taxis) in London. To drive one, you must pass a test, called the Knowledge, to prove you know your way around.

Going underground

From the 1830s, people got about London by train. Then, in 1863, the world's first *underground* line opened, between Paddington Station and Farringdon Street. The carriages were pulled by steam engines, so passengers often became covered in soot. By 1890, the trains had electric motors.

Angel station has the tube network's longest escalator, with a 27.5m (90ft) drop.

This poster, from 1910, encourages Londoners to travel by the Underground.

Today there are around 270 London Underground stations, although half of them are actually above ground. Around 3 million people travel between the stations every day.

London Underground is often known as 'the Tube', because of the round tunnels that many of the trains travel through.

River traffic

In the 19th century, hundreds of steam ferries carried people between busy docks up and down the Thames. The river often became clogged with all the traffic. But, as more railways were built, fewer Londoners chose to travel by boat.

Today, some people still get to work on boats. Speedy *Thames Clippers* whisk them along the river.

This 19th century painting shows how crowded the Thames became, as a ferry passes between moored ships and boats.

Victorian steam ferries had tall funnels, which were lowered when the boats passed beneath bridges.

Index

Usborne Quicklinks

For links to websites where you can find out more about London, go to the Usborne Quicklinks website at www.usborne.com/quicklinks and type in the title of this book. We recommend that children are supervised while using the internet.

Acknowledgements

Cover: Nelson's Column © ImageState/Alamy; London Eye © Robert Gates/Alamy; Tower of London painting © Akg-images/Ullstein Bild; Palace guard © Imagebroker/Alamy; **The beginning...** Roman London © Museum of London/Peter Froste; Gladiator helmet © The Art Archive/Musée Archéologique Naples/Gianni Dagli Orti; Mosaic © The Trustees of the British Museum; Boudicca © 2016. Photo Scala, Florence/Heritage Images; Model of Old St Paul's Cathedral © Museum of London; Guildhall © Granville Davies/Alamy; Guild sign © Museum of London; **Westminster Abbey:** Procession of the Knights of Bath © by courtesy of Dean & Chapter of Westminster Abbey, UK/The Bridgeman Art Library Nationality; Door carving © James Brunker UK/Alamy; Coronation of Henry IV © Lebrecht Music and Arts Photo Library/Alamy; Coronation Chair © Angelo Hornak/Alamy; Henry III window © Mark Fiennes/The Bridgeman Art Library Nationality; Tomb of Unknown Warrior © Angelo Hornak/Corbis; Poet's Corner © James Brittain/The Bridgeman Art Library Nationality; **Tudor Times:** Map of London © Private Collection/The Stapleton Collection/The Bridgeman Art Library Nationality; St. James's Palace © Eric Nathan /Alamy; Shakespeare's Globe © Anne-Marie Palmer/Alamy; Shakespeare portrait © Alfredo Dagli Orti/The Art Archive/Corbis; Golden Hinde © John Farmar/Alamy; Tavern sign © Museum of London; Jewelled scented bottle © Museum of London; **The Tower of London:** Tower of London painting © Akg-images/Ullstein Bild; Lady Jane Grey © National Gallery, London, UK/The Bridgeman Art Library Nationality; Execution block © Peter Titmuss/Alamy; Raven © Jim Zipp/Science Photo Library; Beefeater © Clay Perry/Corbis; Silver engraved armour of Henry VIII © Royal Armouries, Leeds, UK/Bridgeman Images; Imperial Crown of India © Anwar Hussein Wire Image/Getty Images; **Plague & Fire:** Plague cartoon © Sheila Terry/Science Photo Library; Plague doctor © Akg-images; Bill of mortality © Private Collection/The Bridgeman Art Library Nationality; Plague bell © Museum of London; Great Fire painting © Museum of London; The Monument © Berni-Vent/Alamy; The Golden Boy © Justin Kase z13z/Alamy; **After the Fire:** View of London © Museum of London; Silk dress © Museum of London; Doll's house © Museum of London; Lord Mayor's Coach © Museum of London/the City of London Corporation; Pleasure garden © Museum of London; Night watchman © Museum of London; Newgate © Private Collection/The Bridgeman Art Library Nationality; **Things to see from Georgian London:** Banqueting House © Angelo Hornak/Alamy; Townhouse © Hideo Kurihara/Alamy; Kensington Palace © One-image photography/Alamy; Fortnum & Mason © Holmes Garden Photos/Alamy; Samuel Johnson © Rod Williams/Alamy; St. Bride's © Shangara Singh/Alamy; Temple Bar © Andrew Parker/Alamy; St. James's Park © Colin Palmer Photography/Alamy; **St. Paul's Cathedral:** Canaletto painting © Lobkowicz Palace, Prague Castle, Czech Republic/The Bridgeman Art Library Nationality; St Paul's Cross © Haydn Hansell/Alamy; St. Lawrence Jewry window © ImageState/Alamy; Nelson's tomb © Steppenwolf/Alamy; **Buckingham Palace:** Royal crest © Brian England/Alamy; Palace guard © Imagebroker/Alamy; Marble Arch © UK City Images/Alamy; Royal Standard © Peter Grimmett/Alamy; **Victorian London:** Embankment painting © The Art Archive/Museum of London; Crystal Palace © The Great Exhibition of all Nations, by Chavanne, pub. by Read & Co. (print), French School, (19th century)/Private Collection/The Stapleton Collection/Bridgeman Images; Natural History Museum © Nic Cleave Photography/Alamy; Charles Dickens © Private Collection/The Bridgeman Art Library Nationality; Applicants for admission to the Casual Ward © Topham Picturepoint; Pollution cartoon © The Granger Collection/TopFoto; **Things to see from Victorian London:** Nelson's Column © Skyscan Photolibrary/Alamy; Landseer's Lion © Travelpix/Alamy; National Gallery © RayArt Graphics/Alamy; Temple Bar Memorial © PSL Images/Alamy; Queen Victoria © Tom Joslyn/Alamy; Royal Albert Hall © Justin Kase z12z/Alamy; Albert Memorial © Alistair Laming/Alamy; St. Pancras © Londonstills.com/Alamy; Tower Bridge © Larry Lilac/Alamy; **The Houses of Parliament:** Gunpowder plotters © Mary Evans Picture Library/Alamy; The Burning of the Houses of Lords and Commons © 2016. Photo The Philadelphia Museum of Art/Art Resource/Scala, Florence; Lion statue © David Tomlinson/Alamy; Royal Throne © Angelo Hornak/Corbis; Painted wall panel © Arcaid Images/Alamy; Downing Street © Justin Kase z11z/Alamy; Big Ben © Xiaoyang Liu/Corbis; **London at war:** Recruitment poster © Museum of London; St. Paul's in the Blitz © The Art Archive/Culver Pictures; Evacuate London Poster © Lordprice Collection/Alamy; The Cenotaph © Michael St. Maur Sheil/Corbis; Fire-fighters memorial © Michael K Berman-Wald/Alamy; Spitfire © Ian Andrews/Alamy; HMS Belfast © Alex Segre/Alamy; **London today:** Lloyds Building © DBURKE/Alamy; London Eye © J Marshall-Tribaleye Images/Alamy; 30 St Mary Axe © Prisma Bildagentur AG/Alamy; City Hall © Fionline digitale Bildagentur GmbH/Alamy; Tate Modern © Eric Nathan/Alamy; British Museum © Terry Harris/Alamy; Chinatown © Michael Kemp/Alamy; **London transport:** Garden-seat horse-bus and S-type bus © Tfl from the London Transport Museum collection; Routemaster bus © Getty Images; Black cab © Jonathan Tennant/Alamy; Angel station escalator © AA World Travel Library/Alamy Stock Photo; Underground Poster © Antiques & Collectables/Alamy; Pool of London © Guildhall Library, City of London/The Bridgeman Art Library Nationality; Thames Clipper © Tristar Photos/Alamy

With thanks to Ruth King
Digital manipulation by John Russell and Brian Voakes

First published in 2017 by Usborne Publishing Ltd., Usborne House, 83-85 Saffron Hill, London, EC1N 8RT, England. www.usborne.com Copyright © 2017, 2014, 2012 Usborne Publishing Ltd.